US AIR FORCE
Alphabet Book

JERRY PALLOTTA ★ **SAMMIE GARNETT** ★ Illustrated by **VICKIE FRASER**

iꙮi Charlesbridge

In memory of US Air Force mechanic Uncle Tony Pallotta, who flew real and fake atomic bombs all over the world after World War II.—J. P.

In memory of family and friends Russell O. Large, Jimmy Frank White, Greg Bruce, and Harold Wells. Thank you to my family and friends for bravely serving our nation: Bob Mallory, Nathan Schwamburger, Gary Weitekamp, Jay Neal, Rob Hyde, Ed Hubbard, Dennis Bernia, Mark Postema, Darrell McCall, and James White. In honor of the guys from my hometown, Coeburn, VA: Mickey Marcus, Charles Bemben, Carson Bond, Gene Lundy, Ronnie Miltilton, Bill Hensley, Charles Blanton, Don Lay, Woody Lay, Randy Kilgorem, Clint Lawson, J. B. Steele, J. B. Atwood.—S. G.

Thank you to all the US Air Force officers who assisted in making this book possible.—V. F.

The authors would like to thank the USAF; National USAF Museum; Tyndall Air Force Base; Tyndall AFB Public Affairs; Christen Abner, Robert Barnes, Herman L. Bell, Jonathan Billie, Thomas E. Bonifay, Bryan Bouchard, Matthew Bradley, Gabriel Brooks, Tom Burgess, Kathleen Cordner, Christopher Dahmer, Brian J. Davis, April DeReus, Tracy L. English, Aaron Farrior, Laurent Fox, Matthew Galan, Patrick Gibser, Dave Graff, Paul Hough, Jason C. Kraemer, Ty'Rico Lea, Derrick Lee, Steve Luczynski, Manuel Martinez, Jason Medina, Mike Mistretta Jr., Charles D. Morrow, Lisa Carroll Norman, Marc D. Piccolo, Christopher W. Reel, Larry Reid, Lou Roberts, Jerry Roe, Susan A. Romano, Sean K. Schookover, Abbie South, Harrison Southworth, Andrea Valencia, Abraham Vasquez, Adrian E. Vergara, Judith Wehn, Steven Whiting, David J. Wilson, and Bruce E. Zielsdorf.

Published by Charlesbridge
9 Galen Street • Watertown, MA 02472
(617) 926-0329 • www.charlesbridge.com

Printed in Malaysia
(hc) 10 9 8 7 6 5 4 3 2 1

Illustrations done in mixed media
Display type set in Rockwell by Monotype
Text type set in Memphis by Adobe Systems Inc.
Printed by Papercraft in Johor, Malaysia
Production supervision by Jennifer Most Delaney
Designed by Cathleen Schaad and Ellie Erhart

Special thanks to David Biedrzycki for help with the cover and the letter V artwork. Some images sourced from the Defense Visual Information Distribution Service.

Library of Congress Cataloging-in-Publication Data
Names: Pallotta, Jerry, author. | Garnett, Sammie, author. | Fraser, Vickie, illustrator.
Title: US Air Force alphabet book / Jerry Pallotta, Sammie Garnett, Vickie Fraser.
Other titles: United States Air Force alphabet book
Description: Watertown, MA: Charlesbridge, [2023] | Audience: Ages 4–7 | Audience: Grades K–1 | Summary: "This alphabet book has something about the US Air Force for every letter."—Provided by publisher.
Identifiers: LCCN 2022020789 (print) | LCCN 2022020790 (ebook) | ISBN 9781570919527 (hardcover) | ISBN 9781632897282 (ebook)
Subjects: LCSH: United States. Air Force—Juvenile literature. | Alphabet books—Juvenile literature. | English language—Alphabet—Juvenile literature.
Classification: LCC UG633 .P335 2023 (print) | LCC UG633 (ebook) | DDC 358.400973—dc23/eng/20220427
LC record available at https://lccn.loc.gov/2022020789
LC ebook record available at https://lccn.loc.gov/2022020790

Aa

A is for Air Force. An air force defends its nation from the air. Originally part of the US Army, the Army Air Corps became its own military branch in 1947 and changed its name to the US Air Force (USAF).

Airmen flew bombers such as this B-24 Liberator in World War II.

Bb

B is for Bomber. The US Air Force flies B-2 stealth bombers that are invisible to enemy radar. The swing-wing B-1 Lancer flies low and fast and carries large payloads, or bombs. The B-52 bomber has eight engines.

Cc

C is for Cargo Aircraft.
The C-130 Hercules, C-17 Globemaster, and C-5 Galaxy are giant cargo-carrying aircraft. They deliver military equipment, food, water, and supplies to troops all over the world. They also deliver humanitarian aid to victims of natural disasters.

AIR MOBILITY COMMAND

Dd

D is for Drone. Drones are pilotless aircraft. The MQ-1 Predator and MQ-9 Reaper are remotely controlled from the ground. Drones allow the air force to fly in difficult places or in areas that might endanger pilots' lives.

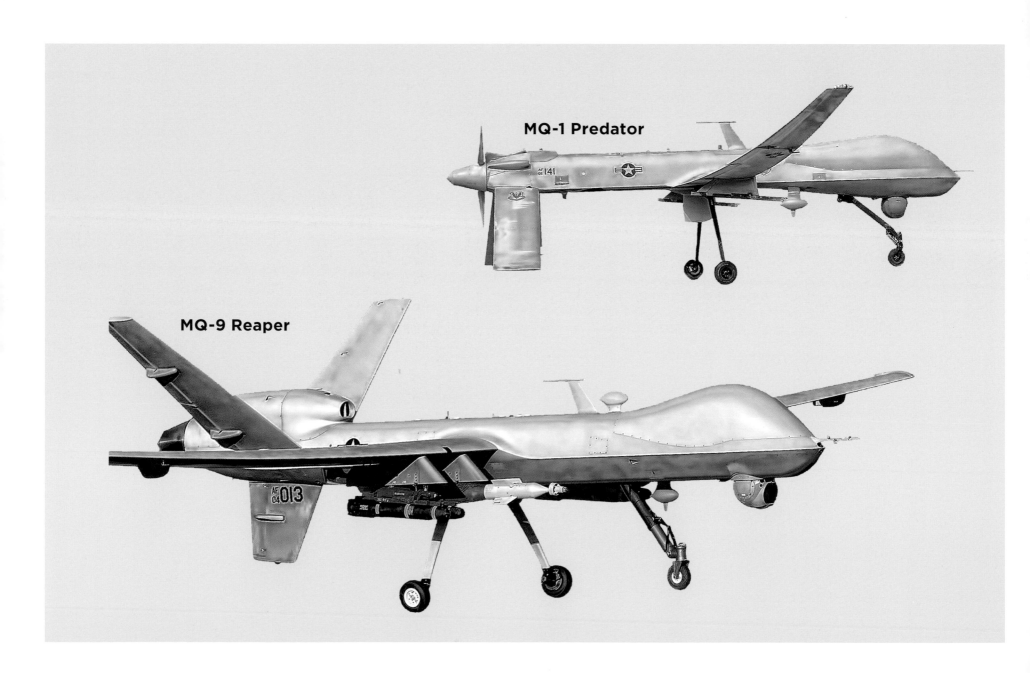

MQ-1 Predator

MQ-9 Reaper

E is for E-3. The E-3 Sentry can see incoming planes and threats in the air from many miles away. It is known as an AWACS, which stands for <u>A</u>irborne <u>W</u>arning <u>A</u>nd <u>C</u>ontrol <u>S</u>ystem. A rotating radar dome on the top of the plane enables it to detect, identify, and track friendly and enemy aircraft.

Ee

Ff

F is for Fighter Jet. An F-15 Eagle can fly almost 2,000 miles per hour. It can soar from New York to Los Angeles in less than two hours. An F-35 is a stealthy fighter that can zoom in on enemies before they know it.

F-15

F-16

F-22

F-35

F-18

An F-16 flies fast, carries powerful weaponry, and is loud! An F-18 has two engines. An F-22 is the best air fighter in the world.

Did You Know?
An air battle between fighter jets is called a dog fight.

Gg

G is for Glider. Gliders are airplanes without engines. In World War II, the Army Air Corps towed gliders filled with soldiers. The planes snuck over enemy lines and landed without a sound. They also carried jeeps and cargo up to 4,000 pounds!

H is for Helicopter. Helicopters are used for secret missions and to rescue stranded pilots. The CV-22 Osprey takes off like a helicopter—straight up—then turns its propellers and flies like an airplane. HH-60G Pave Hawk helicopters recovered NASA's space capsules when they splashed down in the ocean. Today, the UH-1N Huey flies behind enemy lines and performs other important missions.

Ii

I is for Insignia. Rank insignias are badges that air force personnel wear to designate the chain of command. These insignias differentiate officers, sergeants, and airmen from each other. They also wear ribbons and medals to identify battles they have fought and honors they have received.

Did You Know?

The Air Force Cross is the highest honor in the US Air Force.

Insignia	Grade	Rank
	O-1	Second Lieutenant
	O-2	First Lieutenant
	O-3	Captain
	O-4	Major
	O-5	Lieutenant Colonel
	O-6	Colonel
	O-7	Brigadier General
	O-8	Major General
	O-9	Lieutenant General
	O-10	General
	Special	General of the Air Force

Insignia	Grade	Rank
	E-1	Airman Basic
	E-2	Airman
	E-3	Airman First Class
	E-4	Senior Airman
	E-5	Staff Sergeant
	E-6	Technical Sergeant
	E-7	Master Sergeant
	E-8	Senior Master Sergeant
	E-9	Chief Master Sergeant
		First Sergeant
		Command Chief Master Sergeant
		Chief Master Sergeant of the Air Force

J is for Jet Engines. Some aircraft use propellers to fly. A propeller has angled blades that push air. A jet engine burns fuel, which spins fans and forces air out of a smaller hole in the back of the engine. A rocket engine ignites fuel, which propels an aircraft or missile.

Jj

Kk

K is for Knowledge.

The United States Air Force Academy, a four-year military college, is in Colorado Springs, Colorado. Graduates receive a bachelor of science degree and are commissioned as second lieutenants in the USAF.

L is for Lackland Air Force Base. Lackland is known as "the Gateway to the Air Force." After enlisting, recruits attend eight and a half weeks of basic military training at Joint Base San Antonio Lackland. Training includes physical conditioning, classroom instruction, and working as a team.

Mm

M is for Missiles.
Missiles are rocket-propelled explosives. The airmen who work with missiles are called munitions systems specialists.

GBU-39

GBU-32

AIM-9

AIM-120

A-10 WARTHOG

P-40 WARHAWK

N is for Nose Art. Some air force pilots paint on the noses of their planes. Nose-art pictures can look funny or scary. Other nose-art pictures remind pilots of their sweethearts or of movie stars.

Nn

Oo

O is for One. Air Force One is a modified Boeing 747 that carries the president of the United States. It is the flying White House for the president, who is our commander in chief.

Pp

KC-135

KC-10

AC-130 SPECTRE

E-8D JOINT STARS

P is for Planes. The air force flies fighters and bombers but also operates unique aircraft.

- KCs, such as the KC-135 or KC-10, are known as gas stations in the sky. They refuel another plane while both are flying—also known as "passing gas."

- A Spectre can circle over a battle and support our troops that arc fighting on the ground.

- E-8D Joint STARS, a converted passenger plane with a twenty-four-foot-wide radar system that can detect movement on the ground. STARS stands for Surveillance Target Attack Radar System.

The Ernie
WWII Muse
Friends of Ernie
765-665-

Qq

Q is for Quonset Hut. A quonset hut is an easy-to-build shelter with a rounded roof. In years past, the air force built them to house troops, parts, and even airplanes in far-off locations. You can still find old quonset huts in the deserts of Arizona or the snowpacks of Antarctica.

R is for Red Horse. These air force teams fly into combat areas and build airfields. Red Horse stands for Rapid Engineer Deployable Heavy Operational Repair Squadron Engineer. Other teams called Prime Beef (Base Engineer Emergency Force) build barracks. Like the navy's Seabees and the army's combat engineers, Red Horse airmen are both construction civil engineers and fighting soldiers.

Rr

Ss

S is for Space Force. The air force was once in charge of our nation's orbiting military satellites. Today, a new military branch called the United States Space Force manages this part of our defense system. Satellites are used for listening to our enemies, guiding missiles, and helping ships navigate. The US Space Force should have its own alphabet book!

T is for Tuskegee. In World War II, brave African American pilots formed a special air group called the 99th Fighter Squadron. They trained in the small town of Tuskegee, Alabama, and became known as the Tuskegee Airmen. Today they are remembered and honored as courageous pilots who fought with distinction.

Tt

Uu

Uniforms make US Air Force personnel look great but also help them do their jobs. Some uniforms have handy pockets for a pilot's instruments.

Other uniforms are made tough so airmen can wear them for long flights. Which uniform do you like best?

V is for Valkyrie. This supersonic jet was planned to be the meanest, baddest, toughest bomber in the USAF. Powered by six huge rear engines, it was scheduled to carry nuclear weapons. But enemy missile technology made the Valkyrie obsolete. You can still see one at the National Museum of the United States Air Force near Dayton, Ohio.

W is for Weatherbird. Weather is an important factor in a military mission. Pilots called hurricane hunters fly their WC-130J Hercules—also called a weatherbird.

Ww

Xx

X is for X-Craft. The United States began building experimental aircraft, or x-craft, in the 1940s. In 1947, air force hero Chuck Yeager flew an X-1, the first aircraft to break the sound barrier. He named his plane *Glamorous Glennis* after his wife. Later, the X-15 broke other speed barriers, trained pilots to become astronauts, and led to the development of modern jets.

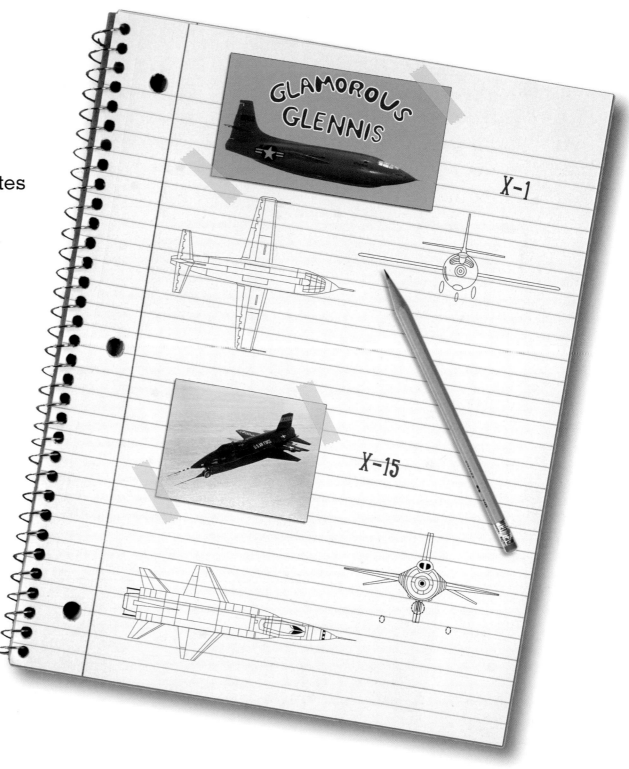

Y is for Yesterday. It seems just like yesterday that Wilbur and Orville Wright were flying kites and building a simple two-winged glider. In 1903 the Wright brothers completed the first powered and controlled manned flight. Only forty-four years later, airmen went from flying a loose collection of bicycle parts and canvas to breaking the sound barrier. Just twenty-two years after that, astronauts landed on the moon in Apollo 11.

Yy

1903

Wright brothers' flight at Kitty Hawk, Dec. 17, 1903

1909

First United States military aircraft delivered

1917

First United States planes flown in combat during WWI

1918

United States Army Air Service formed

1926

United States Army Air Corps formed

1941

United States Army Air Force formed

1947

United States Air Force formed

1969

Airmen flew to the moon in Apollo 11

2021

First helicopter flight on Mars

Zz

Z is for Zulu Time. The air force flies planes across the globe at all times of day and night. Because Earth is divided into twenty-four time zones, air force pilots set their watches to what they call Zulu time, which is based on the time of day in one specific location: the Royal Observatory in Greenwich, England.

MILITARY AIRCRAFT DESIGNATION (MAD)

US Air Force aircraft are named with letters and numbers.
The letters tell the mission or role of each aircraft.
The number stands for the model of each aircraft.

A Attack

B Bomber

C Cargo/Transport

E Special Electronic Installation

F Fighter

H Helicopter

K Tanker

M Multi-mission

O Observation

P Patrol

Q Drone

R Reconnaissance

S Antisubmarine

T Trainer

U Utility

V Vertical takeoff/land

W Weather

X Research

Y Prototype

Integrity first,
Service before self,
Excellence in all we do.

United States Air Force Memorial,
Arlington, Virginia